# God's Word is Food

## *The 90-Day Daily Devotional to Release God's Power for Breaking Strongholds*

**Kimberly Taylor**

TakeBackYourTemple.com

Please see your health care provider for diagnosis and treatment of any medical concerns, and before implementing any nutrition, exercise or other lifestyle changes.

# Table of Contents

# Introduction

*"I have not departed from the commandment of His lips;  I have treasured the words of His mouth More than my necessary food."*

- Job 23:12

When I first read the above scripture while studying a book called *"Exalting His Word"* by Shelley Quinn, I stopped dead in my tracks. Have you ever had one of those "lightning-bolt" experiences when you know something has happened that will change your life forever? Reading that scripture was that kind of moment for me.

After I read it, I had to get real with myself. I had to ask if I, like Job, treasured God's word more than I treasured food.

Mentally I said "Of course I do." But when I looked at the time I spent feeding my body, versus the time I spent feeding my spirit, I was sorely lacking.

Then I thought about how the world views Christians. Many of them see us as hypocrites, saying one thing, but doing another. I had once been that way myself. I started changing as I slowly renewed my identity in Christ through study of God's word. But I knew I could go even deeper.

I asked myself, "What breakthroughs could happen if I began to treasure God's word more than food and demonstrate that love through spending more time in it?"

That's when the title zoomed through my head: *God's Word is Food.*

The Holy Spirit challenged me for 90 days to commit to study God's Word as much or more than I consumed food. It wasn't a legalistic requirement, but instead an exhortation that promised to bring benefits to me far beyond the small amount of time I was investing. You will get the same benefits in this study.

It is unique because it uses the theme of food to give you key principles of victory for your Christian life. I recommend that you don't just do this study once – do it at least once a year because I guarantee every time, you will get new insights from it and your spirit will be renewed.

In the natural, eating the right foods can heal, energize, and nourish you. But eating the wrong foods or starving yourself can make you sick, weak, and drain your energy. It works the same in the spirit. With this challenge, you will have plenty of the right foods to strengthen your spirit so you can make the wise choices necessary to change your life for the better.

Ultimately, your goal as a believer is to reflect God's glory in your life as Jesus did. He revealed God's beauty, truth, and wisdom to others. And you are destined to do the same thing. But you can't do it on your own power. You need His.

If you treasure and consume God's word more than your necessary food for 90 days and apply what you learn, these benefits are yours:

- You will have an abundant life
- Your mind will be transformed.
- You will make your way prosperous and you will have good success.

God promises these benefits if you meditate on His word. It has the power to change lives. I have seen it in my own life, and in the lives of friends, family, and coworkers.

Here is a promise to snack on right now:

*Jesus answered and said to him, "If anyone loves Me, he will keep My word; and My Father will love him, and We will come to him and make Our home with him."*

- *John 14:23*

To be able to keep His word, you need to know what His word says. You'll be eating most of your meals from the book of John with scriptures from other books to complement your meal.

What is on the menu? You'll dine on sparkling water, wine, meat, bread, fruit, fish, and assorted harvest produce.

In this book, you'll find:

- Encouraging scriptures to memorize related to each week's focus topic
- Affirmations to speak to ground your identity in Christ
- Suggested bible passages to study
- Additional resources to enhance your study

To start the challenge, you need to have:

- A bible. I recommend the New King James Version or the New American Standard Bible for its readability
- Index cards - these will come in handy to write focus scriptures on so that you can 'feed' on them throughout the day
- A small notebook  or journal to keep track of the blessings/lessons you are learning as a result of this study
- An open heart and mind, one willing to lay aside unprofitable things in your life and grab hold to what satisfies
- Commitment and willingness to give yourself grace - if you find yourself forgetting to take in

God's Word as you planned, don't beat yourself up. Just grab a bite at your next opportunity and keep going!

At the end of your 90 days, share your testimony to inspire others.

Are you ready to get started with the challenge? I'm excited and I hope you are too. Let's get going!

## Week 1: The Main Course

Congratulations on your commitment to consume God's word more than your necessary food for the next 90 days. For some of you it may be 3 times a day, for some 6 times a day. Right now, decide how often you feel led to consume God's word and when you will do it.

The easiest way to remember to consume your portions of God's Word is to do it before your meal and snack times. You might choose to write a scripture mentioned in this study on an index card and review it throughout the day, read passages that are encouraging to you, or speak scriptures out loud to encourage yourself.

You might listen to a bible on CD or offer up a prayer of thanksgiving. You have many options to eat. Get creative!

By the end of the 90 days, you want the word of God to overflow your heart so much that His words will come out of your mouth. You want to be able to speak to any mountain in your life and be confident that the mountain has to be moved because His word says so!

To get you started in this first week, the first item on the menu is meat, as in the Lamb of God, Jesus.

## Scripture

*But as many as received Him, to them He gave the right to become children of God, to those who believe in His name: who were born, not of blood, nor of the will of the flesh, nor of the will of man, but of God.*

*And the Word became flesh and dwelt among us, and we beheld His glory, the glory as of the only begotten of the Father, full of grace and truth.*

*- John 1: 12-14*

## Affirmation

Say this statement aloud now and at least once every day this week:

*I am a child of God because I believe on the name of His son Jesus. As God's child, I have been given rights to an abundant life. I reflect my Father's beauty, grace, wisdom, and truth in every word that I speak and in everything that I do.*

## Reflection

For our study, we are starting with the book of John. It has one purpose: to give us a picture of Jesus Christ and the works he did on the earth so that we might believe on him and be called the children of God.

Children share in the inheritance of their parents. Some of us received a great inheritance and some a poor one. But when you accepted Jesus as your savior, you hit the jackpot. You were adopted into God's family and accepted as a child of God with all the rights associated with it!

That is why when you approach God, you must always come in the name of Jesus. Only Jesus' righteousness is worthy to have an audience before a Holy God.

Through Jesus' sacrifice on the cross, you have been reconciled into a relationship with God. Jesus made the sacrifice; you accepted His sacrifice by believing on his name. In the Old Testament, lambs were the required sacrifices for people to make amends for their sins.

When Jesus came, he became the lamb sent from God to atone for the sins of the whole world. When he died and rose again, the Old Testament sacrifices were no longer required. All that was required was for us to confess our sins before God and accept Jesus as our savior.

If you have accepted Jesus as your savior, consider this: You have already done the most important thing in life. Everything else that you accomplish after that is just a bonus!

During this week's study, reflect on God's forgiveness and grace in sending Jesus to atone for our sins. According to 1 John 1:9, all we need to do now is to confess our sins, and He is faithful and just to forgive us our sins and to cleanse us from all unrighteousness.

Are there any sins or strongholds that you need to be freed from in your life right now?

If you are not sure, then model what David asked for in Psalm 139:23: "Search me, O God, and know my heart; Try me, and know my anxieties." You might also review the works of the flesh as described in Galatians 5: 19-21 for guidance in this area.

And when God reveals the sin or stronghold to you, be quick to confess it in prayer. Ask for His forgiveness and power to turn from it. Ask for Him to give you a complete change of heart and mind in that area of weakness. Through this, He will be glorified.

God is rich in love, goodness, grace, and mercy. Once you confess, receive His forgiveness and reflect in gratitude that your restoration is possible only because of the loving sacrifice of the Lamb of God.

## Study & Meditation

John Chapter 1

Day 1: John 1: 1-5
Day 2: John 1: 6-13
Day 3: John 1: 14-18
Day 4: John 1: 19-28
Day 5: John 1: 29-34
Day 6: John 1: 35-42
Day 7: John 1: 43-49

## Questions for further study

1. In Psalm 139:23, David pleaded with God: "Search me, O God, and know my heart; Try me, and know my anxieties."

2. What sins/strongholds are causing you anxiety in your life right now? *food addiction*

3. How would your life change without these anxiety-causing circumstances? *I could move easier, I'd feel better.*

4. How can you invite Jesus' cleansing power into your life right now to free you from these circumstances and restore your peace of mind? *prayer, reading & studying the Word*

## Week 1 Tip: Speaking the Word into your circumstances

Here is a tip to assist you in the God's Word is Food challenge this week: Speak God's word into your situation today.

This week, we are discussing Jesus' role in restoring us into a right relationship with God so that we may be called children of God. As God's children, our ultimate goal is for someone to look at the way we live and say, "Wow they look just like their daddy!"

According to Romans 4:17, one of the things our Father does is call those things which do not exist as though they did.

I put this to the test recently. I was working on a big project and was quite nervous about it. I had a conference call coming up and wanted to be sure my ideas came across well. The closer the time came for the call, the more nervous I got. I tried reasoning with myself to calm my nerves but that didn't help.

Finally, I started speaking the following scripture aloud:

> In God (I will praise His word),
> In the LORD (I will praise His word),
> In God I have put my trust;

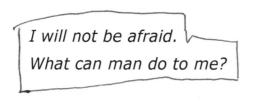

*I will not be afraid.*

*What can man do to me?*

- Psalm 56:10-11

When the time for the conference call came, not only was I calm but the situation turned out completely in my favor! I am convinced it was because I spoke God's word into that situation and rebuked the enemy that was trying to overcome me with a spirit of fear.

If you are facing a challenge in your life right now, have you tried speaking God's word into it?

Your spoken word has power. Try this: in your head, start counting. While you are counting in your head, start speaking Psalm 23 aloud:

*"The Lord is my shepherd, I shall not want."*

Did the counting in your head stop when you started speaking? Of course it did. Your thoughts must always stop to listen when you speak.

So please be **very** careful about what you say. I AM are the most powerful words in the universe because it is the name of our God (Exodus 3:14). So when you say "I am..." be sure the words you are calling yourself are ones you want to answer to.

Likewise, be sure that you are calling your circumstances as you want them to be, not as they are. You aren't ignoring your circumstances but you recognize that your Father is bigger than any circumstance you have.

That is why I include affirmations in the *God's Word is Food* challenge. If you speak them often enough (at least once a day, but several times a day is better), your thoughts will begin to line up with your words. And as you change your thoughts, you change your actions. Only when your actions change do your results change.

And someday soon, others will point to you and say, "Wow, they look just like their Daddy!"

So get ready for some circumstances to start changing!

## Week 2: Water into Wine

Still sticking to your commitment to consume God's word more than food for 90 days? If so, terrific! If not, then now is a perfect time to recommit to the effort. It is easy to allow "life" to get in the way of nurturing your spiritual side.

Without nurturing your spiritual side several times a day, there is no way for you to live the way God would have you live. Jesus made his sacrifice so that we would have an abundant life, a life rich in his goodness, grace and mercy.

That is cause for celebration, don't you think? And that celebration calls for Wine, the next item on the menu.

This week's study comes from John, chapters 2 and 3: *Water into Wine*.

## Scripture

*Now by this we know that we know Him, if we keep His commandments. He who says, "I know Him," and does not keep His commandments, is a liar, and the truth is not in him. But whoever keeps His word, truly the love of God is perfected in him. By this we know that we are in Him. He who says he abides in Him ought himself also to walk just as He walked.*

- 1 John 2:3-6 (New King James Version)

## Affirmation

Say this statement aloud now and at least once every day this week:

*I am a child of God. I keep His word and the love of God is perfected within me. The Spirit empowers me to live according to the principles that Jesus himself taught: I love the Lord with all my heart, mind, soul and strength and love my neighbor as myself.*

## Reflection

What does a life of celebration look like to you? Is it one of gratitude for what you have? Is it making full use of the time God has given you? Is it showing appreciation for those people whom God has placed in your life?

In the book of John, Chapter 2: 1-11, we read the story of Jesus' first miracle of turning water into wine. I've often wondered why that was his first miracle. Why didn't he start with a big healing crusade or a tour of tombs, calling dead people to life out of them, like he did with Lazarus?

I think it is because God wanted the first miracle to show the expected change in a believer's life once Jesus becomes a part of it. Once you have true fellowship with Jesus, you are never the same.

Now I have to admit when I first accepted Jesus as my savior, I did not change the way I lived. Sure, I went to church on Sunday and sang the songs. I could even quote a few scriptures to impress my fellow church members. But my heart was far from Him the rest of the week.

I continued in relationships I had no business being in, wasn't above gossiping or cursing people behind their backs, and blamed others for my problems. It was only after attending a women's conference many years afterward that I learned that accepting Jesus as Savior was just the beginning.

He wanted Lordship over my daily life. That meant living according to the same principles He taught and gaining the same fellowship with the Father as He had.

It was tough admitting that my way of living wasn't working. It was only by getting a vision of the life God had in store for me, one full of purpose, joy, and love that I was willing to throw my hands up and say, "Your will be done."

My watered-down, unhappy life was changed into a full-bodied one of enjoyment.

With my new life, I had to throw some things out. I had to throw out unhealthy relationships, destructive habits, envy, and ungratefulness.

As you read further in chapter 2 of John, you see Jesus had to throw things out too. In the story in which he cleansed the temple, he didn't gently negotiate with the moneychangers to get them to leave. He didn't plead and he didn't tiptoe around them. He drove them out in dramatic fashion because they did not belong there. The moneychangers' presence was a distraction to the temple's true purpose.

I think that many of us can't have the rich life God wants to give us because we've got too many moneychangers (strongholds) up in there! Your strongholds might be like mine: disobedience, destructive habits, a contentious attitude. Here are some questions to consider:

- Are you demonstrating that you love the Lord with all your heart, mind, soul, and strength through obedience to His word? *No. But I want to.*

- How do you treat your neighbor...not only your literal neighbor, but your co-workers, fellow church members, and family members? *I treat other people well*

- Are you nursing destructive habits in your life, like alcohol, drug, food abuse, or sexual immorality? *food abuse – YES*

If your answer is "no", "not good", and "yes," it is time to allow the indwelling of the Spirit to turn water into wine in your own life. Here are some awesome promises to consume:

- If you abide in Me, and My words abide in you, you will ask what you desire, and it shall be done for you (John 15:7).

- For God has not given us a spirit of fear, but of power and of love and of a sound mind. (2 Timothy 1:7)


- I can do all things through Christ who strengthens me. (Philippians 4:13)


If you've got some strongholds in your life that are contrary to God's ways, then focus on abiding in Him by keeping His word. Pray and ask for the help you need in every moment when faced with choices to feed your spirit (walk in the way Jesus walked) or feed your stronghold (act according to your old habits). Speak the above promises into your situation.


Develop a keen awareness of each moment of the day and ask yourself, am I honoring God in the way I'm acting (or speaking) right now? As you allow the spirit's power to change you, then get ready to experience a life that you can savor...just like a fine wine.

## Study & Meditation

John Chapter 2, 1 John Chapter 2

Day 1: John 2:1-12
Day 2: John 2:13-25
Day 3: 1 John 2:1-11
Day 4: 1 John 2:12-14
Day 5: 1 John 2:15-17
Day 6: 1 John 2:18-23
Day 7: 1 John 2: 24-29

## Questions for further study

1. What does a life that honors God look like to you? *Generous, honest, the fruit of the spirit, good, decent person*

2. We all struggle with loving our neighbors as ourselves. How can you demonstrate love to your neighbor in the way you speak and act? *be welcoming & glaerous*

3. In what areas do you need to ask the Holy Spirit for help in living a life of obedience to God's word? *my food addiction primarily also to be more forgiving + less judgemental*

## Week 2 Tip: Living a New Life

Here is a tip to assist you in the God's Word is Food challenge: Live your life knowing that you are a new person today.

In the book '*Execution: The Discipline of Getting Things Done,*' the authors said that the one skill that separates successful companies from unsuccessful ones is the ability to execute. The word *Execute* has two meanings: one meaning is to put to death and the other is to perform fully. When I thought about the meaning of execute in the Christian life, two scriptures immediately came to mind:

*Therefore we were buried with Him through baptism into death, that just as Christ was raised from the dead by the glory of the Father, even so we also should walk in newness of life.*

- Romans 6:4

*I have been crucified with Christ; it is no longer I who live, but Christ lives in me; and the life which I now live in the flesh I live by faith in the Son of God, who loved me and gave Himself for me.*

- Galatians 2:20

As a believer in Christ, your old nature is dead. Through Christ, you are given a new life. What does that life look like for you? Write that down and resolve to walk in it.

You've made mistakes in the past? So what! There is nothing you can do about the past. But you change your present and positively impact your future.

Today say, "It is no longer I who live, but Christ lives in me." And then focus on execution, putting to death those thoughts and actions that oppose your new life, performing fully those things that do. And a fully, richer life will be yours!

## Week 3: Living Water

Have you ever had a glass of cool water on a hot day? How refreshing it is! When you receive Jesus as your savior, He promises that you will receive living water and that you will never have to thirst again. In other words, you will have everything that you need to sustain life. That is a wonderful promise! Let's take a drink of that water right now in this week's lesson.

This week's study comes from John, chapter 4: *Living Water*.

## Scripture

*Jesus answered and said to her, "If you knew the gift of God, and who it is who says to you, 'Give Me a drink,' you would have asked Him, and He would have given you living water."*

- John 4:10 (New King James Version)

## Affirmation

Say this statement aloud now and at least once every day this week:

> *I possess abundant gifts from God. I have a personal relationship with Him through His son, Jesus Christ. In God's very name, I AM, is the promise of His presence in any situation I am facing. I have the spirit of truth inside of me and I have His word by which to live. I am blessed because my delight is in the law of the LORD, and on His law I meditate day and night. I am like a tree planted by streams of water, which yields its fruit in season and whose leaf does not wither. Whatever I do prospers.*

## Reflection

Modern life is like a desert and the cares of this world drain us dry. We worry about crime, out of control gas and food prices, job instability. But you don't have to be drained. You don't have to worry or be anxious. God Himself has given us the means to refresh ourselves and gain strength: through the living water of His presence and relationship with Him.

I was reflecting on this as I was reading the story of how God first appeared to Moses in the burning bush (Exodus Chapter 3).

After God told Moses who He was, He gave Moses a job to do – to bring God's people out of Egypt. Moses immediately asked, "Who am I that I should go to Pharaoh?" God didn't even bothering answering the question. Instead God reminded Moses of who He was.

I thought about God's name of "I AM". I AM is the promise of God's presence. God always was, God is, and God ever shall be. It doesn't matter who you are. It doesn't matter what your circumstances are.

What matters is I AM.

- I AM is the source of your identity
- I AM is the source of your confidence
- I AM is the source of your faith
- I AM is the source of your peace
- I AM is the source of your job
- I AM is the source of your strength
- I AM is the source of your deliverance
- I AM is the source of your health
- I AM is the source of your finances
- I AM is the source of your relationships
- I AM is the source of your life

Many of us do not experience victory in our lives because we are living with a spiritual trickle when abundance is available. When we are feeling thirsty for God, I AM is there. All we have to do is focus on His name, His character, and ask that we be filled with His spirit. He will pour it out on us to overflowing.

In Jeremiah 2:13, the prophet (speaking of Israel) says: *"My people have committed two sins: They have forsaken me, the spring of living water, and have dug their own cisterns, broken cisterns that cannot hold water."*

Are you seeking for security and fulfillment apart from God? Are you seeking it in material possessions, addictions, or in a relationship? That is the same as attempting to dig your own cistern as the Israelites did. And like them, you will find that this approach doesn't hold water.

But if you choose to recognize the awesome promise of I AM, turn to God, and regularly seek Him in personal relationship, you are assured that you are in God and He is in you.

I was sharing the previous reflection with my husband Mike, and he added a contribution that makes this lesson even more powerful. He said this regarding when you use "I am" to refer to yourself:

When you think of "I am" as "I AM," which is God himself, it takes on new power and strength. You possess the strengths of God because God is in you:

- "I AM" the creation of God (I am in God, the creation of God)
- "I AM" the child of God  (I am in God, the child of God)
- "I AM" loved by God (I am in God, loved by God)
- "I AM" blessed by God  (I am in God, blessed by God)
- "I AM" known by God (I am in God, known by God)
- "I AM" visited by God daily (I am in God, visited by God daily)
- "I AM" under God's divine protection (I am in God, under God's divine protection)
- "I AM" educated by God (I am in God, educated by God)

Wow! There is power in His name and power in His presence! With a personal relationship with God, you are promised the following:

*"But blessed is the man who trusts in the LORD, whose confidence is in him. He will be like a tree planted by the water that sends out its roots by the stream. It does not fear when heat comes;*

*its leaves are always green. It has no worries in a year of drought and never fails to bear fruit"* (Jeremiah 17:7-8).

Today, focus on God's name of I AM. It is all sufficient for you. Reflect on His character (Exodus 33:12 - Exodus 34: 9 is a great place to start).

Resolve to set aside regular time to commune with God through study of His word. It is as essential to your spiritual life as water is to your physical life.

## Study & Meditation

John Chapter 4

Day 1: John 4:1-14

Day 2: John 4:15-26

Day 3: John 4:27-42

Day 4: John 4:43-54

Day 5: Psalms 1:1-6

Day 6: Jeremiah 17:5-8

Day 7: Isaiah 55: 1-2

## Questions for further study

1. In what things have you sought security apart from God in the past? *through relationships food & sex*

2. How would your life change if you grounded your identity in God? *it would change everything for the better. Help me to do this my Lord*

3. How can you ensure that you set aside time everyday to regularly commune with God?

*Do it first thing in the morning. Before anything else.*

## Week 3 Tip: Build Up Faith with Video

Although it's still early in your challenge, I hope that you're starting to see benefits already from your study. Here's another tip that can help you consume God's word regularly: watching Bible study videos on the Internet.

I discovered this when I was exercising using the jump rope. Usually I will watch a television program to keep my mind occupied during my exercise time, but I got a bright idea. Why not search Google videos to see if there were any recorded materials that would help me further my studies and that I could watch while I was jumping?

One of my favorite Bible stories is the one about how Moses led the Israelites from Egypt, so I was looking for a video study on the book of Exodus.

I discovered a wealth of information on that site! You can also search for other videos at Google videos using the keywords "Google Video Bible study" or you can search for particular book of the Bible to see what is available.

I'd like to congratulate you too for making this commitment. I know that you will see many continued blessings from it. Keep going and may God continue to richly bless you!

## Week 4: An Abundant Harvest

We're fast coming up on one month of your challenge and I hope you're enjoying your meals! I know I have. I have more peace and confidence within, and things that used to stress me don't anymore. By nurturing my spirit, I am reaping a good harvest.

Since most food must be planted and harvested before it can be brought to the table, we're going to discuss the concept of the harvest in this week's lesson.

Our study continues from John Chapter 4: *A Harvest of Abundance.*

## Scripture

*Jesus said to them, "My food is to do the will of Him who sent Me, and to finish His work."*

- John 4:34 (New King James Version)

## Affirmation

Say this statement aloud now and at least once every day this week:

*As a child of God, my food is to do the will of my Father. I sow to the Spirit in my thoughts, words, and actions and reap an abundant harvest of love, joy, peace, and self control. I sow words of encouragement and support to friends, coworkers, and family members and reap stronger, more satisfying relationships as a result.*

## Reflection

Eating is one of life's great pleasures. But unless you are living off a diet of animal products only, you are eating food that someone took the time to plant and harvest. In John Chapter 4:31-36, we see that the disciples were trying to get Jesus to eat, but he told them that his food is to do the will of his Father who sent him.

You know how it feels to eat a good meal, particularly when you are hungry. You feel deep satisfaction, contentment, and nourished after you're fed properly. That same sense of deep satisfaction can be had by being obedient to God's word and will daily.

One of the things God wants us to do as believers is draw others into the kingdom. We do that by the seeds we sow into our own hearts through study of God's word and the seeds we sow into other people's lives. Take a moment to think about the seeds you are planting right now.

1. Are you planting as much word into your heart through diligent study and meditation as you could be?

2. When you go into work, can people tell that you are a follower of Christ by the way you act?

3. At home, do you demonstrate the love of Christ to your spouse and family?

4. Are you as patient with your children when they makes mistakes as God is with you?

If you need some work in these areas, now is the time to rededicate yourself to planting! Plant more seeds of God's word into your heart. Give a smile, a kind word, or offer to help someone who needs it. Not only will you be doing the will of your Father, but you will reap blessings yourself and enjoy the harvest of an abundant life.

## Study & Meditation

Reflections on the Harvest – Scriptures from Leviticus, Psalm, Proverbs, and Matthew

Day 1: Leviticus 26: 3-12

Day 2: Psalm 107: 1-9

Day 3: Psalm 107: 33-38

Day 4: Proverbs 6:6-11

Day 5: Matthew 9:35-38

Day 6: Matthew 13:1-9

Day 7: Matthew 13: 18-23

## Questions for further study

A key biblical principle is that of sowing and reaping. Take a moment to reflect on your life and circumstances right now.

1. In what areas are you satisfied with the harvest that you are getting?

2. In what areas are you dissatisfied with the harvest that you are getting?

3. In those areas in which you are dissatisfied, what seeds can you sow today that will ensure you will have a better harvest tomorrow?

## Week 4 Tip: Renewing Meditation

Here's another quick tip that can help you consume God's word regularly: Meditate regularly as instructed in God's word.

The world teaches that meditation is sitting with your legs crossed, eyes closed, and chanting. The goal with this type of meditation is emptying your mind.

But people of faith are taught differently. Instead of emptying our minds, we are instructed to fill them. We think deeply about God's word, savor it, and allow our minds to make  connections on how to apply it to our daily lives. God promises that when we renew our minds, we are transformed.

From the bible, here is some wisdom about meditation:

Joshua 1:8

*This Book of the Law shall not depart from your mouth, but you shall meditate in it day and night, that you may observe to do according to all that is written in it. For then you will make your way prosperous, and then you will have good success.*

Psalm 63:6

*When I remember You on my bed, I meditate on You in the night watches.*

Psalm 77:6

*I call to remembrance my song in the night; I meditate within my heart, And my spirit makes diligent search.*

Psalm 77:12

*I will also meditate on all Your work, And talk of Your deeds.*

Psalm 119:27

*Make me understand the way of Your precepts; So shall I meditate on Your wonderful works.*

Today, consider some ways you can include this practice to help you with the challenge. You will renew your mind and be empowered to live according to God's will and way.

## Week 5: More Than Enough

Have you ever had those times in your life when you wondered how you were going to make it? You were low on physical or financial resources. Well, the disciples faced just such a situation. But what they found out was that Jesus had an answer for them to supply their need. And that's what you'll discover in this study too.

This week's study comes from John, chapter 6: 1-14: *More than Enough*.

## Scripture

*And my God shall supply all your need according to His riches in glory by Christ Jesus.*

- Philippians 4:19 (New King James Version)

## Affirmation

Say this statement aloud now and at least once every day this week:

*I trust God completely to supply all my needs, spiritually, physically, emotionally, and financially. He has promised to supply all my needs according to His riches and glory in Christ Jesus. I believe Him. God is not a man that He should lie nor a son of man that He should repent. God has said and He will do. God has spoken and He will make it good. As I wait patiently on Him, I allow patience to have her perfect work so that I may be complete, lacking nothing. I thank God for supplying all of my needs this day.*

## Reflection

John Chapter 6:1-14 tells the familiar story of how Jesus feed 5,000 men with only 5 barley loves and 2 small fish. The disciples were clearly concerned about the situation as we all would have been. In the natural, there is no way you can feed that many people with so little!

But by the time Jesus intervened in the situation, the crowd was not only well fed, but there were even 12 basketfuls of barley loaf fragments left over.

Let's look at the process Jesus used here to supply the need:

1.  He recognized the need.

2.    He saw what was already available in the natural to deal with it.


3.    He thanked God for what He had.


4.    He distributed what He had to others and saw God supernaturally multiply it.


    We can use this same process to handle any needs that we currently have. The first thing is to recognize that we have a need and to take it to God in prayer.


    We pray to God consistently about it. Even though God hears you the first time, the persistent prayer grows your faith, which pleases Him.


    Secondly, ask yourself what resources you have to deal with the situation. If it is an emotional issue like depression, is there a support group or friend that you can lean on for help? If a financial situation, do you need financial counseling to help manage your money more effectively?

Next, be thankful. Always have an attitude of praise for what you have. If God has provided you with shelter, food, and the basic necessities of life, that is plenty to be thankful for.

Finally, share what you have with others. If you are depressed, try sharing a smile and offering to help someone else. If a financial issue, can you invest a talent you have to earn extra income to help pay the bills? Ask God to multiply your effort for a return that not only meets your need, but gives you more than enough.

And then get ready! Just as Jesus knew that God was more than able to supply the need in spite of circumstance, you will discover the same and that God delights in His role as our provider – our *Jehovah Jireh*.

## Study & Meditation

John Chapter 6:1-14 (with support from Luke, Exodus, and 2 Kings)

Encouragement on how God supplies all needs:

    Day 1: John 6:1-14 (Physical Healing)

    Day 2: John 5:1-15 (Physical Healing)

    Day 3: Luke 8: 26:29 (Mental Healing)

    Day 4: Luke 15: 11-32 (Lost Family Member)

Day 5: Exodus 16: 1-16 (Food)

Day 6: Exodus 16: 17-36 (Food)

Day 7: 2 Kings 4: 1-7 (Financial Need)

## Questions for further study

1. What needs do you have right now?

2. What resources do you have in the natural to deal with these needs?

3. What are you grateful to God for in this situation?

4. What things can you ask God to supernaturally multiply to take care of your needs?

## Week 5 Tip: Finding Time to Eat

Are you finding it hard to find time to consume God's word regularly?  Here's another tip that can help you with the challenge: pre-planning your day the evening before.

This simple time management tip saves me much time and stress. Simply get a small notebook and create a list of everything you want to accomplish the next day. In addition to work-related things, you want to be sure to list things that contribute to your overall wellbeing, like exercise and prayer time.

Interestingly enough, doing the planning first thing in the morning didn't work nearly as well for me as doing it the evening/night before. It was almost as if during the night, my brain mentally prepared for what I had to do and thought of creative ways to get the tasks done easier and faster.

The next day, you want to make sure that the things you do first are those that are most important to you - either the things that would have the biggest long-term benefit for you or those that would have serious consequences if you don't do them.

Cross things off the list as they are completed. If you didn't get to a task that day, move it to the next day until it gets done.

The cool thing about this technique is the feeling of accomplishment it gives. You can see in black and white evidence that you did something that moved you closer to your goals that day. It should give you more time to study God's word too.

## Week 6: Bread from Heaven

We are now at the half-way point of the challenge and I hope you are feeling full of God's Word! Is it renewing your mind, coming forth from your mouth? If not, sounds like you may need to eat some more spiritual food.

May I suggest having some bread? It's one of the basic food groups. The bread I'm talking about is not the bread stripped of nutrition like the world gives. It is the hearty kind that is full of things that heal, energize and nourish you. So let's break some bread together.

This week's study comes from John, chapter 6: 22-40: *Bread from Heaven*

## Scripture

*"And Jesus said to them, 'I am the bread of life. He who comes to me shall never hunger, and he who believes in Me shall never thirst.'"*

- John 6:35

## Affirmation

Say this statement aloud now and at least once every day this week:

*I'm done settling for less. I am ready for the best! God gave me His best when He sent His son Jesus to die for me. Through Him I have eternal, abundant life. My spirit is full of him and as I walk in the spirit, I never hunger and I never thirst. He is the true bread of heaven and I eat of this bread always.*

## Reflection

In John 6, a crowd had just witnessed Jesus performing a miracle, feeding five thousand people with just five barley loaves and two fish. Yet they asked for a further sign that they might believe in him.

They mentioned how God had provided manna, bread from heaven, to sustain their ancestors in the desert after their exodus from Egypt. But Jesus corrected them and said that He is the true bread of heaven. And unlike earthly bread that spoils, His bread is eternal.

Romans 14:17 reminds us that the kingdom of God is not eating and drinking but righteousness, peace, and joy in the Holy Spirit. As you walk with Jesus by studying his life and living the Word, you will experience fullness of life that you have never had before.

Just think of living the world's way as like consuming white bread. It's colorless, flavorless, plus the life-giving nutrients have been removed and replaced with inferior imitations.

But living God's way through life in Christ is like eating delicious multigrain bread - it is deep in color, rich in flavor, and bursting with vitamins and minerals that help you function at your best. Which bread are you choosing every day?

Are you settling for less when God wants to give you the best? Let today be the day that you upgrade your intake and start eating your share of the bread of heaven. You will find that it is tasty food indeed!

## Study & Meditation

John 6: 22-40, with support from Exodus

Day 1: John 6:22-27

Day 2: John 6:28-33

Day 3: John 6:34-40

Day 4: Exodus 16:1-5

Day 5: Exodus 16:6-12

Day 6: Exodus 16:13-26

Day 7: Exodus 16:27-36

## Questions for further study

1. In what ways do you think you have settled for less in your life?

2. What things can you do this week to demonstrate that you are ready for the best?

## Week 6 Tip: Raise Your Expectations

In this week's lesson, I asked if you are settling for less when God wants to give you the best. Here's another tip that can help you with the challenge: raise your expectations.

Raising your expectations is an expression of faith. Faith is simply confidence that God keeps his promises. I love to read Deuteronomy 28 because it outlines the blessings of obedience that God promises to believers. I want those promises in my life and I expect God to fulfill those promises to me as I obey him.

So I recommend that you read Deuteronomy 28 and other biblical promises and write down what you are expecting from God based on those promises. And then, read those expectations every day. You will be amazed at how doing this will strengthen your faith and fill you with great joy.

To give you an example, here are a few expectations that I wrote, which my husband and I agreed upon concerning our lives. Use these as a model to create your own expectations list:

- We expect God's constant and continual presence, protection, provision, and prosperity in and around our lives and those of our families and friends.

- We expect all currently unsaved family members to accept Jesus as their personal savior.

- We expect the fulfillment of all the blessings of Deuteronomy 28 in our lives as we obey God.

- We expect the Holy Spirit to empower us to obey the voice of the Lord our God and to enable us to keep His commandments forever so that we may obtain the blessings of Deuteronomy 28.

- We expect that because we obey and serve God forever, we shall spend our days in prosperity, and our years in pleasures.

- We expect the Holy Spirit to guide us into all truth; for He speaks not on His own authority, but whatever He hears He speaks; and He tells us things to come.

- We expect a long, extraordinary, joyful, fruitful marriage all the days of our lives and to raise our children in the fear and admonition of the Lord, children who glorify the Lord and honor their parents.

- We expect that we prosper and are in health as our soul prospers all the days of our lives.

- We expect restoration and maintenance of our youthful vigor, vitality, energy, strength, and flexibility.

- We expect that when we go home to be with the Lord, He will say to us, "Well done, thy good and faithful servants. Enter into the joy of your Lord."

I pray these expectations bless you and will encourage you too to raise your expectations of God and see what mighty things He will accomplish in your life as you obey and serve Him!

## Week 7: Flesh and Blood

Up until this point, we've had some good food, haven't we? Some bread, some wine, some fish...all appealing foods. So you might be shocked to find out what's on the menu this week. Even the disciples back in Jesus' day didn't want to eat it. But this food is foundational to the Christian faith: Jesus' flesh and blood. And this is the most precious food of all.

This week's study comes from John, chapter 6: 41-71: *Flesh and Blood*

## Scripture

*"For My flesh is food indeed, and My blood is drink indeed. He who eats My flesh and drinks My blood abides in Me, and I in him. As the living Father sent Me, and I live because of the Father, so he who feeds on Me will live because of Me."*

- John 6:55-57

## Affirmation

Say this statement aloud now and at least once every day this week:

> *My identity is anchored in Christ Jesus. I believe that Jesus is the son of God and died to save me from my sins. I share in his resurrection and have received new life through Him. I abide in him and he abides in me. I am worth nothing less than the price he paid for me.*

## Reflection

In the latter part of John chapter 6, the disciples received a hard saying from Jesus. He told them that unless they ate his flesh and drank his blood, they would have no life in them. If you were living back then, wouldn't you have been shocked at this statement? You might have wondered if Jesus was encouraging you to become a cannibal!

But of course Jesus was speaking figuratively. He was saying that to receive abundant life, they would have to take him in.

That is exactly what happened in your life. When you accepted Jesus s your Savior, you said "Yes!" to him. You invited him to come in to your life, save you from your sins, and become a permanent part of you. Jesus is your literal flesh and blood!

When you remember that his body was broken for you, you take in his flesh. When you remember that his blood was shed for you, you take in his blood.

Throughout the Old Testament, God taught His people that life was in the blood. The fact that Jesus sacrificed his life for you means that he saw you as worthy of the price he paid. When he shed his blood for you, he gave you his life.

So this week, I ask you to anchor your identity in Christ Jesus. Remember his sacrifice for you and the great love he has for you. Every time you have feelings of unworthiness or low self esteem, see that as a spiritual hunger signal. You need to nourish yourself on Jesus' flesh and blood. Remember, reflect, rejoice! And you will be revived.

## Study & Meditation

John 6: 41-71, with support from Leviticus, Matthew, Mark, and 1 Corinthians

Day 1: Leviticus 17:11-14

Day 2: John 6:41-51

Day 3: John 6:52-59

Day 4: John 6:60-71

Day 5: Matthew 26:26-30

Day 6: Mark 14:22-26

Day 7: 1 Corinthians 11:23-36

## Questions for further study

1. What have been the consequences if you have experienced feelings of low self-esteem and unworthiness in the past?

2. Since you know that Jesus gave his life for you, what does that say about your life?

3. Since you know that Jesus loves you, how can you show that same love to yourself and others?

## Week 7 Tip: Strengthen Yourself in Joy

Think about the last time you watched the evening news. At the end of the broadcast, did you feel stronger and uplifted? Probably not. If fact, you probably felt tired, weighed down from the troubles of the world.

But I recommend instead to strengthen yourself regularly in God's good news. So here's another tip that can help you with the challenge: Strengthening yourself in joy.

Most of us say that we want to be happy. But happiness is unstable because it is tied to your circumstances. If things are going well, you are happy. If things are going poorly, you are not. But joy is a constant state of being. You can be joyful no matter what is going on around you.

What is the source of this joy? Walking with God. Living in righteousness. Obeying God's word.

Here are some scriptures to meditate on concerning joy so you can strengthen yourself whenever you are feeling weary:

- Nehemiah 8:10: *"Do not sorrow, for the joy of the LORD is your strength."*

- Psalm 5:11: *"But let all those rejoice who put their trust in You; Let them ever shout for joy, because You defend them; Let those also who love Your name Be joyful in You."*

- Psalm 16:11: *"You will show me the path of life; In Your presence is fullness of joy; At Your right hand are pleasures forevermore."*

- Isaiah 61:10: *"I will greatly rejoice in the LORD, My soul shall be joyful in my God; For He has clothed me with the garments of salvation, He has covered me with the robe of righteousness, As a bridegroom decks himself with ornaments, And as a bride adorns herself with her jewels."*

- Psalm 126:5: *"Those who sow in tears; Shall reap in joy."*

So today, resolve to be strong in the Lord and in the power of his might - by focusing on the joy of your growing relationship with Him!

## Week 8: A Grain of Wheat

This lesson deals with a word that is not really popular in Christian life: sacrifice. After all, it conjures of images of discomfort, even pain.

But Jesus puts a different spin on sacrifice by using the simple image of a grain of wheat falling to the ground. Let's take a closer look at this grain of wheat and how the principle of sacrifice can bring forth an abundant life for us.

This week's study comes from John, chapter 12: 20-26: *A Grain of Wheat*

## Scripture

*"He who loves his life will lose it, and he who hates his life in this world will keep it for eternal life."*

- John 12:25

## Affirmation

Say this statement aloud now and at least once every day this week:

> *I have been crucified with Christ; it is no longer I who live, but Christ lives in me; and the life which I now live in the flesh I live by faith in the Son of God, who loved me and gave Himself for me.*

## Reflection

In John chapter 12: 20-26, Jesus used a grain of wheat to illustrate the principle of sacrifice. He said that a grain of wheat must fall to the ground and die in order for it to bring forth even more grain.

Sacrifice is giving up something of lesser value to gain something of greater value.

Jesus goes on to say that if someone loves his life in the world, he will lose it, but those who lose their lives for his sake will find it.

The way I interpret that is, if you are committed to preserving your old way of doing things, then you will lose out on the fulfilling life Jesus died to give you. However, if you lose your life (give up your old way of doing things), then you will save it because you learn to live in newness of life with him.

As a person of faith, one of the greatest lessons to learn is that your life is not your own. Once you accept Christ, you no longer belong to yourself because Jesus bought you at a very high price - his sinless life. So you gladly give up your so-called "right" to the things that you used to do.

Thankfully, the empowering of the Holy Spirit enables you to do what feels unnatural.

That's what Jesus' sacrifice and resurrection was all about! He promised that he would send His disciples a helper after His return to the Father in heaven.

That same Holy Spirit lives inside of each believer in Jesus today - empowering us to live God's way. All you have to do is make a decision, giving up those worldly things of low value - destructive habits and negative emotions come to mind - and gain something of greater value. You will agree that peace and fellowship with God is worth the sacrifice.

## Study & Meditation

John 12: 20-26, with support from Galatians

    Day 1: John 12: 20-26

    Day 2: John 12: 27-36

    Day 3: John 12: 37-41

    Day 4: John 12: 42-50

    Day 5: Galatians 2:11-21

    Day 6: Galatians 3:1-9

    Day 7: Galatians 3:10-18

## Questions for further study

In the reflection, sacrifice was defined as giving up something of lesser value to gain something of greater value.

1. What "lesser value" items in your life do you need to give up?

2. What will you gain when you make this sacrifice?

3. Do you think making this sacrifice will impact your relationship with God? In what way?

## Week 8 Tip: Be Bold!

Here's another quick tip that can help you with the challenge: Start being bold!

In Luke 18: 1-8, Jesus tells the parable of an unjust judge who was continually beseeched by a widow for him to give her justice from her adversary. The judge only gave her justice because she kept coming to him, being persistent in her request. Jesus gave us this parable to show how we should pray to God continually and not lose heart.

This reminds me of an incident recently with my four year-old niece. She had been given a toy chemistry set as a present and she wanted me to play with her. I was in the middle of completing a project and told her "I will play with you, but give me just a minute."

However every couple of minutes, she would come back to me and ask, "Are you ready to play now?" I had to smile. Her boldness and persistence were amazing. She did not give up asking me until I stopped to play with her. For me, it was a relief to be able to do so at last!

So it pleases God when we are persistent and bold with our prayers. In 1 Thessalonians 5: 17, we are told that praying without ceasing is the will of God in Christ Jesus for us.

We are also told in Hebrews 4:16 that we are to come boldly to the throne of grace that we may obtain mercy and find grace to help in time of need. So if you are being hesitant in your prayer life, then start being bold.

Since you are studying the word of God in earnest now, you can have greater confidence that your prayers line up with His word.

And you can be sure that in God's good timing, He will perform His word as He has promised.

## Week 9: Life in the Vineyard

This lesson contains the ultimate secret of a successful Christian life. A bold statement to be sure, but once you get this principle and practice it in your daily life, you will NEVER be the same. So let's take a stroll in the most beautiful vineyard you will ever see and eat of its luscious fruit.

This week's study comes from John, chapter 15: 1-8: *Life in the Vineyard*

## Scripture

*"Abide in Me, and I in you. As the branch cannot bear fruit of itself, unless it abides in the vine, neither can you, unless you abide in Me."*

- John 15:4

## Affirmation

Say this statement aloud now and at least once every day this week:

> *Without constant fellowship with Jesus Christ, I can do nothing. With Him, I can do everything God calls me to do! I abide in Jesus and he abides in me. My life is hidden in him and I bear much fruit. By this, my Father is glorified.*

## Reflection

Have you ever known someone who professed to be a Christian but their behavior was anything but Christ-like? I have to admit that I was once such a person.

I had accepted Jesus as my savior in my late 20s but nothing really changed in how I lived. I was just as judgmental, selfish, and prideful as I ever was.

It took a remarkable weekend at a Christian women's retreat to experience God's love personally. During that weekend, away from my normal routine, I was able to focus on God, his word and bask in His constant presence.

For the first time in my Christian life, I was abiding in Christ. It was intoxicating and I haven't been the same since! Once I got a taste of the good stuff, the cheap vintage was no longer satisfying.

I can see a real difference in how I handle life when I am diligent about practicing the presence of God through prayer, praise, worship, and study of his word. I feel truly alive and grounded. However, if I allow life to get in the way of my fellowship with God, I feel dry and my relationships suffer.

So having experienced that personally, now I know why people of the world sometimes cannot tell the difference in someone who professes Christ versus someone who does not. If a person does not nurture a connection with God through Christ daily, then they will be unfruitful. That relationship is your source, your lifeline.

You want to become so fruitful that people in the world will see your fruit and say, "Wow, I want some of that!"

Because this scripture is so foundational to Christian life, I am going to take the unusual step of asking you to read the same scripture three days in a row. It is that important. So this week, practice abiding in Christ and allow the scripture to really sink into your spirit. I promise you that you too will experience new richness in Christ!

## Study & Meditation

John 15: 1-8 (repeated), with support from Genesis, Psalm, and Jeremiah

Day 1: John 15: 1-8
Day 2: John 15: 1-8
Day 3: John 15: 1-8
Day 4: Genesis 1: 26-28
Day 5: Psalm 1: 1-3
Day 6: Psalm 128: 1-6
Day 7: Jeremiah 17:5-8

## Question for further study

1. What steps can I take this week to abide in Christ at a deeper level than I have been?

## Week 9 Tip: Nutshell Bible Studies

Here is another quick tip that can help you consume God's word regularly: Review "nutshell bible studies."

A great strategy is to ingest the bible in bite-sized pieces when you are short on time. I discovered a terrific resource that helps you do just that at raystedman.org.

Although Pastor Stedman has gone home to be with the Lord, he has left behind a treasury of free bible studies from almost every book of the bible. The studies are gleaned from Pastor Stedman's 40 years of preaching.

In addition to this resource, you can do a search for "devotional" on Google for just about every scripture.

So check out the nutshell bible lessons and you will agree that this is a great way to keep consuming God's word as you enter the last weeks of your challenge.

## Week 10: Savoring Your Meal

Last week, I shared with you the ultimate secret of a successful Christian life. But later in John 15 is, in my view, the most outrageous, wonderful promise God makes to those who believe in Him.

This promise is so incredible that you might find it difficult to believe. But I want you to really meditate on the implications of this promise and I truly hope that you will apply it to your life immediately.

So let's linger in the vineyard and savor the fruit of this promise.

This week's study comes again from John, chapter 15: 1-8, with laser focus on verses 7-8.

## Scripture

*"If you abide in Me, and My words abide in you, you will ask what you desire, and it shall be done for you. By this My Father is glorified, that*

*you bear much fruit; so you will be My disciples."*

- John 15:7-8

## Affirmation

Say this statement aloud now and at least once every day this week:

*Because I abide in Christ and his word abides in me, I ask for what I desire according to God's word and will, and it is done for me. Standing on this promise, I have confidence that all of my prayers are answered in God's perfect timing.*

## Reflection

Do you get excited saying the above affirmation? I do! It is a great testament to God's love for his children. He wants to equip us with every good thing that we need to accomplish His purposes on this earth.

I recently got a great lesson on this principle. I participated in a 10-K road race and struck up a conversation with an older gentleman as we waited for the race start. He was a lawyer and talked about his son and daughter with great affection.

He was telling me how his daughter was in graduate school and how he had paid for her to go to college and grad school. He had done the same thing for his son. He said that he was so glad that he had the resources to be able to do this, and his pleasure was apparent.

Not having had the benefit of an earthly father's love or provision, I greatly admired this father's dedication to making his children's lives better. Then I remembered the following scripture from Matthew 7:7-11:

*"Ask, and it will be given to you; seek, and you will find; knock, and it will be opened to you. For everyone who asks receives, and he who seeks finds, and to him who knocks it will be opened. Or what man is there among you who, if his son asks for bread, will give him a stone? Or if he asks for a fish, will he give him a serpent? If you then, being evil, know how to give good gifts to your children, how much more will your Father who is in heaven give good things to those who ask Him!"*

Now this man did not claim Christ in any shape or form, yet he knew how to give great gifts to his children! But you have a heavenly Father who is able to give far beyond what this earthly father can.

So the question is...are you abiding in Christ, allowing his words to penetrate your heart and then...asking God for what you desire according to his word and will?

If you are not, then you are leaving behind untold gifts God wants to give you.

So start abiding, studying, and asking. And start praising as you receive the gifts your Father has reserved just for you.

## Study & Meditation

John 15: 1-8 (repeated on this last day), with support from Matthew and Luke

Day 1: Matthew 7:7-14

Day 2: Matthew 7:15-23

Day 3: Matthew 7:24-29

Day 4: Luke 11:1-4

Day 5: Luke 11:5-8

Day 6: Luke 11:9-13; Luke 11:27-28

Day 7: John 15: 1-8

## Questions for further study

1. Now that I know if I abide in Jesus and his words abide in me, I can ask God for what I desire and it will be done for me, what will I now ask God for?

2. What has stopped me in the past from making requests of God?

3. On what basis can I be assured that God will answer my request?

# Week 10 Tip: Building God Confidence

Here is another quick tip that can help you consume God's word regularly: Focus on Building God Confidence.

In the self-help movement, motivational speakers often talk about how important it is to build your self-confidence and self-esteem for ultimate success in life. However, that type of confidence is unstable by its very nature.

A better plan is to have *God confidence*. God is all powerful, all-seeing, and never changes.

To build God confidence this week, here are a few passages I suggest you study:

- Exodus 34:5-7: Moses boldly asked God to reveal His glory to him, and God passed His goodness before Moses, describing His character as He did so.

- Joshua, Chapter 6: God revealed His unique and effective battle strategy to Joshua for conquering the city of Jericho.

- Daniel Chapter 3: Shadrach, Meshach, and Abed-Nego express ultimate God confidence in the midst of a fiery trial.

Happy building!

## Week 11: Juicy Fruits

Wow, we are really enjoying ourselves in the vineyard, aren't we? The food is so good here. First, you learned the ultimate secret of Christian life, which is abiding in Christ and allowing Him to live out his life through you. Then you discovered the ultimate promise God makes to believers - if you abide in Jesus and his word abides in you, you may ask what you desire and it will be done for you.

Now you are about to feast on the fruits of a life in Christ. I think you will agree that these are some juicy morsels and once you taste them, you will never want to go back to the way you once lived.

This week's study comes again from John, chapter 15: 9-17, with laser focus on verses 16-17.

## Scripture

*"You did not choose Me, but I chose you and appointed you that you should go and bear fruit, and that your fruit should remain, that whatever you ask the Father in My name He may give you. These things I command you, that you love one another."*

- John 15:16

## Affirmation

Say this statement aloud now and at least once every day this week:

*I am an appointed disciple of Jesus Christ. Because I am his disciple, I study his word diligently so that I may bear much fruit. Evidence that I am abiding in Christ are fruits of love, joy, peace, patience, kindness, goodness, faithfulness, gentleness and self control. However, if I experience worry, depression, envy, jealousy, hatred, addictive behavior, outbursts of anger, or other negative behaviors, from now on I will see these as a warning signal that I have stepped outside of my savior's care. In that moment I will again anchor myself in Jesus through his word and invite him to abide in me so that he may take control and renew me with his spirit.*

## Reflection

You are chosen. Doesn't it make you feel good to know that Jesus personally picked you to be one of his disciples? I know it makes me feel good to know that he loves me in spite of all my imperfections. But the great thing is that he loves me too much to leave me exactly as I am.

He appointed you and me so that we may be forever changed and become a shining reflection of him through the fruits we bear in our lives.

And what are these fruits? Love, joy, peace, patience, kindness, goodness, faithfulness, gentleness and self control. I hunger to experience more of these fruits in my own life and I know you do too. I've always found it wonderful that Jesus didn't say that others will know I am his by how big my bible is, how many bible verses I can quote, or how loudly I pray. He said that others will know that I am his disciple by my love. In fact, in John 15: 17 he commands all believers to love others.

The reason for this is obvious: God is love and when you love others, you allow God to show His love for them through you. Haven't you found that you respond far better to another person's love than their lecture? So when you demonstrate the love of Christ to others and show the fruits of your fellowship with him, you are in a far better position to witness about the benefits of a life in him.

The fruits of living in him are so good you won't want to keep it to yourself - this is food you definitely want to share!

## Study & Meditation

John 15: 9-17 (repeated on this last day), with support from other verses from John, Psalm, and Galatians

Day 1: John 13: 1-17

Day 2: John 13: 31-35

Day 3: Psalm 32: 6-11

Day 4: John 14: 19-24

Day 5: John 14: 25-31

Day 6: Galatians 5:13-26

Day 7: John 15: 9-17

## Questions for further study

Based on Galatians 5:13-26, what fruits am I bringing forth in my life?

1. Am I satisfied with these fruits?

2. What fruits do I need to ask the Holy Spirit to cultivate more in me?

3. What fruits do I need to ask the Holy Spirit to prune in me?

## Week 11 Tip: Allowing God to Speak First

Here's another quick tip that can help you with the challenge: Allow God to speak first in your prayer time.

Have you ever noticed how noisy modern life is? Television...iPod...cell phones...computer games. It seems that we often can't even hear ourselves think! The downside to all of this noise is that we often can't hear God speak to us either.

Until recently, I always approached my prayer time with an agenda. I went into my prayer closet with my bible and two books that contain prayers and affirmations. I prayed, spoke my affirmation and then would be quiet for a little while to see if God would speak to me.

But one day, the Holy Spirit told me to leave my books behind and take only the bible. And when I started to speak as usual, I heard clearly "Shut up." So I did, lay down and was just quiet. In my mind, I said "Speak Lord."

I waited for a while but eventually, the Lord spoke to my heart and ministered to my soul. A few times, I'd find my mind wandering to the cares of the day, but I patiently directed my focus back to Him. When I got up, I felt refreshed, energized. What an amazing thing to put aside my own agenda and seek the Lord on His!

As my husband said later when I told him this story, it was a good thing because allowing God to speak first shows wisdom and respect for Him.

So I ask you: Are you doing what I used to do in my prayer time? Try flipping the script and allowing God to speak first. I will bet that you will experience what I did:

*"But those who wait on the LORD Shall renew their strength; They shall mount up with wings like eagles, They shall run and not be weary, They shall walk and not faint."*

- Isaiah 40:31

# Week 12: Breakfast by the Sea

In this final week of the God's Word is Food Challenge, we are leaving the vineyard and traveling ahead to enjoy breakfast with Jesus by the sea, just as the disciples did. Can you imagine feasting on a breakfast that Jesus himself prepares? Yum!

At this breakfast, Jesus not only showed the disciples personally how he provides more than enough to meet their needs but he also gave them instruction as to what he expected them to do after the meal. And he gives us the same marching orders.

This week's study comes again from John, chapter 21: 1-19.

## Scripture

*"He said to him the third time, 'Simon, son of Jonah, do you love Me?' Peter was grieved because He said to him the third time, 'Do you love Me?'*

*And he said to Him, 'Lord, You know all things; You know that I love You.'*

*Jesus said to him, 'Feed My sheep.'*

- John 21:17

## Affirmation

Say this statement aloud now and at least once every day this week:

> *I am an appointed disciple of Jesus Christ and I love him. Because I love him I obey his command to feed his sheep, who are my brothers and sisters in Christ. I realize that I can only care for them to the degree that I remain in Jesus' love and feed continually on his word. From this time forward, I will do these things and so receive his abundant provision to do all that he calls me to do.*

## Reflection

Before we discuss the breakfast by the sea, let me brief summarize what happened in the chapters before. The events were pretty intense. Jesus told the disciples that he was going away to the Father, was arrested, convicted, and crucified. It was a dark time for his disciples. But we know that wasn't the end of the story, for Jesus did something that was quite remarkable.

He rose from the dead to live again, showing himself to the jubilant disciples. He even allowed doubting Thomas to touch his crucifixion wounds to prove he was real.

So in this final chapter of John, Jesus is with his disciples and they go fishing. The disciples had been out all night but caught nothing. Jesus said to them to cast their nets on the right side of the boat and they would catch some fish. But they didn't just catch some...they caught so much fish that they could hardly bring the net back into the boat!

That is the way it is when we obey God. We often get more than we expect or deserve. The return may not be immediate and it might not come exactly the way we thought it would, but the return is always for our ultimate good.

And even more valuable than God's provision is His presence. We get to fellowship with Him just as Jesus did when he sat on the seashore and prepared bread and grilled fish for his disciples for breakfast.

Now what should come after eating a meal? Activity. Food, while it tastes good, is not given to you primarily to tickle your taste buds. It's main job is to give you the energy you need to accomplish your God-given purpose.

In like manner, the spiritual food you have enjoyed in this challenge thus far is given to you so that you would use it to feed others.

You may feed others through sharing your testimony of what God has done for you, by leading others into a relationship with God through Christ, through volunteering at your church, or simply through a smile or word of encouragement.

In whatever manner God leads you to feed others, do it. And they too will experience the truth of this scripture: "For He satisfies the longing soul, And fills the hungry soul with goodness." – Psalm 107:9

**Study & Meditation**

John 21, with support from other verses from John
> Day 1: John 16: 15-16
> Day 2: John 16: 17-24
> Day 3: John 16: 25-33
> Day 4: John 17: 20-26

Day 5: John 20:10-30

Day 6: John 21:1-14

Day 7: John 21:15-25

## Question for further study

1. How can I feed my brothers and sisters with the food I have received from this challenge?

## Congratulations! Let's Get Moving

Congratulations! You have completed the 'God's Word is Food' 90-day Challenge! I hope you have enjoyed reading these messages as much as I enjoyed writing them. I have been transformed through the study and I hope you have too.

But this is not over yet...it is just the beginning of your renewed life in Christ. I want to share with you the following testimonial from a wonderful woman named Rosanne who was kind enough to share her thoughts upon starting the challenge:

Kim,

I don't know if you will receive this personally but I am driven to write. I just started the readings and God wanted me to let you know how I felt it is EXACTLY what I have needed. Please forgive my typing but I broke my right hand and wrist and am experiencing some arthritic pain to boot.

Anyway, these scriptures have helped me to see how Jesus talks to us through His Word. I was struggling reading the Bible but now really feeling touched.  I am different because of this--God bless you for all you are doing.


Rosanne M.

--Rome, NY


I pray you have an even greater testimony to share since you have completed the challenge. If you do, send me an email at *kimf@takebackyourtemple.com*. I would love to hear your testimony.


Again, congratulations and thank you for enjoying these meals with me for the last 3 months!

## About the Author

*"Just wanted to again thank you for sharing your unique and engaging presentation to help us take back our temples! You were truly a blessing and I know that many were enlightened by what you shared."*

- *Danese Turner, Marietta GA*

When it comes to obesity issues, many speakers are like travel agents; they can tell you where to go, but have never been there. But Kimberly Taylor has the wisdom of a tour guide. Not only has she experienced the struggles of obesity firsthand, but she can help others get out of the diet pit—and stay out for life!

Kimberly Taylor has 15 years of health education and training experience through formal nursing practice (as an R.N. for many years) and research on the relationship between nutrition, physical activity, and chronic disease.

Kim's weight loss success story has been featured in *Prevention Magazine* (August 2008), *Charisma Magazine*, the *Atlanta Journal/Constitution*, and many other magazines and newspapers. She has also been interviewed for *The 700 Club* on CBN, *Essence Magazine*, and various radio programs.

Kim has a heart for others who struggle with weight and debt...once 240 pounds, a size 22, and in $19,000 worth of credit card debt, she can testify of God's goodness and healing power in these areas. Desperate to change her debt situation, she took a Crown Ministries (crown.org) course to learn how to manage money from a biblical perspective.

She used its principles to pay off her debt, and then used her new discipline to implement healthy eating and exercise habits. She was then able to achieve and maintain her ideal weight. This experience prompted her to establish **Take Back Your Temple**, whose title asks God to take control of your body and your life so He can use them for His purpose and agenda.

Kim's exhorts people of faith to become good stewards of all the resources God has given to them, including time, money, talents, and physical health. "I am passionate about empowering others to adopt healthy lifestyles so they can fulfill their God-given purpose," she says.

"My dream is for God's people to stand apart because we are healthy, prosperous and living the abundant life to which we are called. I want non-believers to look at us and want what we have: financial, spiritual, mental, and physical wholeness. Then when they ask us what we are doing differently, we can tell them about Jesus, the author and finisher of our faith.

Made in the USA
Columbia, SC
03 July 2022

62740837R00061